INSIDE SKY BLUE

BY

BUCK DAVIS

MASTERPIECE
(The Echoes of War)

The Echoes of War
  Are frightening to hear
    Enough to send blood pouring
      Through a damaged ear

The Guns roaring wildly
  Made men panic and run
    To see so many dying
      When their lives had hardly begun

The Cries for a Medic
  Echoes up and down the Glen
    But the knowledge of death
      Means nothing to warring men

They hate kill and destroy
  Everything that is alive
    Knowing it is anything goes
      Just to survive

Sure everyone helps their buddies
  But their chances are as good as yours
    Knowing later you must be able
      To tend your own sores

Because they may be badly wounded
  Or possibly already dead
    So mentally you try not to get involved
      You need nothing but the Echoes of War
      in your head

Ask anyone that know
    That is more than enough
        In War death is common
            You have to be tough

Or you do not return home
    You die in a foreign land
        So you do not expect sympathy
            Or go looking for a helping hand

Like yesterday for an example
    Jones and Foster got blown away
        You can not afford tight friends
            When none of us might not see another day

If they are afraid of enemy contact
    And something particular they want to know
        Give them your best advice
            To Find Cover and Fire Low

When and If they should die
    On some lonesome Trail
        You know something was missing
            Asking yourself – Where did I fail

For I am their leader
    Trying to protect them even as they sleep
        And when one gets himself killed
            With dry eyes I always weep

I ask GOD
    Why must this be
        Do these young men have to die
            For this damned nation to remain free

If this is True
   It is a very high price
      To see them fall charging a hill
         Or crossing an open field of rice

We walk all day
   Looking to sleep where We can
      Facing a dedicated foe
         I face him as a Man

Always pushing forward
   Never to Retreat
      Victory is Our ultimate mission
         Vowing never to surrender or accept defeat

Then comes new replacements at last
   There is tears in a Trooper's Eye
      He looks to see if I have a soul and says
         Sarge I don't want to die

I want to see my family
   I want to be returned home
      These are hard moments
         When leaders stand all alone

I have to make him a machine
   Teach him to attack and kill
      And if the enemy don't harm him
         For not fighting maybe I will

I have to teach him how to stay alive
   Also prepare him for his own death
      Emphasizing he is to continue to fight
         Until he draws his last breath

Knowing later to his family
    The dreaded letter I must write
        Explaining how he died
            His dedication to continue to fight

How he charged single-handed
    A machine gun nest
        Yes Maam – Your Son
            Was one of America's Best

He said to tell his mother
    To kneel down and pray
        For his buddies
            Who are still fighting everyday

He wanted her to know he really tried
    To be a Man away from home
        He didn't want her to know he cried
            Because he was afraid to die alone

He said ask her for me Sarge
    Did she receive my last letter
        Asking her to pray
            For things to get better

And how is father
    Is he still hobbling around on his stick
        Has the farm gone to ruins
            Now that he is sick

My little sister
    Who is just entering High School
        Ask her if she still think
            I am a Patriotic Fool

Tell my little brother to stay in the books
    Even if he doesn't like math
        Become a farmer like dad
            Just so he doesn't follow my path

Explain my death to her Sarge
    I don't want Mama to cry
        Tell her as a soldier doing his duty
            It came my time to die

On that trail full of death
    On some soon to be forgotten hill
        Your Son said his Prayers
            Before he finally lay still

Where your son fell
    I pushed on
        When I returned to his remains
            The machine gun was gone

Now I too am shot
    Lying beside him in the mud
        Looking down at my body
            Half covered with blood

I do not know why it was him
    That was not spared
        It could have been me
            Some higher power must have cared

When one of my men die
    A part of me dies too
        How can I relate this to a civilian
            What else can any of us do

I offered myself
  To our enemy guns
    They paid with their lives
      For the death of American Sons

I am a professional soldier
  Killing is the name of the game
    Facing an opponent
      Whose ideals are the the same

I am under Orders to fight
  I am prepared to die
    I kill the enemy where I find him
      Without questioning my superiors as to why

I love The Echoes of War
  Sizzling through my ear
    The eyes of the World are on us
      Because We are here

America asked US to carry Her Colors
  We are holding Them very high
    For this Noble Cause
      We are also prepared to die

What else is there to say
  I know this doesn't sound like it's right
    But wounded or not
      I have to get back to the fight

Maybe I can spare another mother
  From what you are going through
    It is not heroics Maam
      It is what the situation tells me to do

The Real Hero is coming Home
   We are sending Him back to you
      He died as an American Fighting Man
         To The Corp his heart was true

I have to go now
   If you can keep in touch
      You have five hundred thousand other sons over
      here
         They love you like their own or just as much

P.S. Don't know what day it is, no one does

                        Cold Steel, Point Man
                        B Company, 2/327 Infantry Battalion
                        1st Brigade, 101st Airborne Infantry
                        Division – The Republic of South
                        Viet Nam – Hue Province
                        Tet Offensive – February 1968

Hello:

Welcome to the Insides of Sky Blue. For years friends and relatives have asked me to share my writings. I did share a few. But seeing them hurt, crippled and maimed through criticisms of my deficiencies in the mechanics of metaphor and rhyme, made me more protective.

I am not of English descent. I use the English language as best as I can. My own true language was stolen from my ancestors... My writings are not in the same league with English academic majors. My writings are inspired from the center of my being. They come of their own volition. I am merely the recipient of an exchange, whose source is far greater than I can aspire to be. So to have this remarkable source challenged, belittled, or held under critical acclaim, I sheltered them in secrecy. Only sharing them with people whom I thought the message was for.

Some of my writings I can identify with readily. Others are what I call empathetic writings. At some point in time I have felt or was told a particular situation existed, and having been buried in my unconscious with latent effect, a poem eventually emerges.

It is my hope that my station in life will not influence your personal clarity in what is being said. I am in prison for a crime I did not commit. But I committed so many others, it is only poetic justice so to speak. My writings began in Viet Nam in 1968, while engaged in a battle. My first poem " Masterpiece " was published in 1976 by Gainsville Poetry Association, in a book titled " Poetic Horizons ".

There are things I could tell you of each individual poem. But I think it would spoil your objectivity. Therefore I am presenting some of my writings and will let them stand on their own merit. Each one is a reality unto Itself. I am a Poet by chance, not choice. They come and I record them, or some of them. If I am caught without pen and paper, only I will ever know of Its existence. I can't bring back an inspiration.

So come with me into the reality my root of being exposes to hungry minds. Become a spectator as I fight dragons to erase mental blocks and stumbling blocks of the sense organs. Come laugh with me, cry with me and sigh with me as We explore the different realms of day to day life.

I salute you with Love, Peace, and a Cry for Unity.

CONTENTS

A SPECIAL DEDICATION

TO

"AUNTIE"
(Mrs. I. Ceo)

Who once told me, "A hero is one who holds on one minute longer."

ILLEGITIMATE SANCTIONS

Heaven walks between us
   When our paths are straight
   As we attempt to come together
In our present human state

We as two separate entities
   United socially as one
   Totally dependent upon each other
With varying amounts of what our labor has won

Embracing illegitimate sanctions of power brokers
   Applying them to everyone as a whole
   In the form of capitalism communism and socialism
Blind to universal laws as they unfold

From the viewpoint of Socrates
   These realities of economics is unsound
   Natural resources should not be a stepping stone
Nor used to hold another man down

All there is of me
   Can easily be found in you
   Except different journeys into inherited thoughts
Promoting the need to be rich and have beggars too

BUCK DAVIS

"FERTILITY"

INEVITABLY – TIME'S APPRECIATION
STRETCHING ALONG THE MOMENTUM OF ACTUALITY
CREATED A PURE ENTITY
THROUGH THE PROCESS OF NATURAL SELECTION

ENDOWED WITH THE MAGNETIC RHAPSODY
THAT GENERATES MOTION
PAYING HOMAGE TO ETERNAL EVOLUTION
IN UNISON WITH ALL THERE HAS EVER BEEN
OR EVER WILL BE

EMPOWERING THE TRUE RECIPIENT
THE SOLE BENEFICIARY AND HEIRESS
TO BENEVOLENT ASPIRATIONS OF LIFE
AND ALL INFINITE SOURCES THEREIN

BEYOND NARCISSISTIC MINDS IN EXISTENCE
THAT OFFER NO DESIGNATED INQUISITION
OR PERPETUAL RENDITION
OF THE SAME EVER AGAIN

TO THE AGELESS KEEPER OF MIRACULOUS WONDERS
A NON-CUPATIVE DECREE
THE IRREPRODUCIBLE
THE NON-PAREIL

THE ONLY REASON FOR SELF-ABNEGATION
AND DEVOTION OF ABSOLUTE WILL
THE CLIMATIC BUDDING OF LIFE'S RESOLVE
BEFORE   THE   BEGINNING   OF   DESTINED
DETERIORATION

AND THE UNIVERSES AS MAY ATTEND
WILL LIE HUMBLE TO HER NEARNESS
KNEELING BESIDE HER THOUGHTS
WITNESSING ONCE IN A WORLD CHANCE PHENOMENA

BUCK DAVIS

THE ISLES OF COGNITION

THE DISTORTION OF HISTORY
DOES NOT MAKE THE TALE TRUE
THE ESOTERIC RAMBLING OF PHILOSOPHIES
INTRODUCES THE KNOWN UNKNOWN AND
HYPOTHETICAL VIEW

ANCIENTLY REACHING FROM THE IMMEDIATE PAST
TO BE VIEWED IN THEIR PHYSICAL SENSE
THE ENORMITY IS BROADENED
THE UNVEILED TRUTH IMMENSE

WHY WOULD A PERSON RUN AWAY
FROM A SHADOW ON A WALL
WHY WOULD A PERSON STRAIN TO HEAR MOVEMENT
NO MATTER HOW SMALL

WHAT GOOD IS A BROOM
WHEN THERE IS NO DUST
WHAT DISGUISE DOES LOVERS WEAR
WHEN THERE IS NO TRUST

FEAR IS BORN TO A WRONG DEED OR THOUGHT
YET TO BE EXPOSED
A CHAPTER OF UNWORTHINESS
YET TO BE CLOSED

IT BREEDS EVILLY
AS IT REFASHIONS THE HEART AND SOUL
INTO A PICTURE BOOK LIKENESS
OF WHAT IT DOES NOT WANT TOLD

LISTEN TO THE SINGER OF SAD SONGS
AS HE RELIVES AN UNFORGOTTEN PAIN
PETITIONS TO THE MURMURING OF INNER VOICES
ABOUT LOSING AN ILL GOTTEN GAIN

LOOK TO THE SINGER OF SWEET SONGS
THEY WEAR A SMILE IN THEIR MIND
THERE IS NO FEAR OF GHOSTS
TO COME CHARGING UP FROM BEHIND

THESE HAVE LIVED LIFE
ENJOYING THE BEST OF THE GOOD
THEY WANT TOMORROW TO BE NO BETTER THAN
YESTERDAY
IF ONLY IT COULD

LISTENING BECOMES A PRACTICED ART FORM
WHEN YOU HEAR WHAT ISN'T BEING SAID
IN BETWEEN THE ISLES OF COGNITION
WHERE TRUTH IS BEING CONSTANTLY FED

BUCK DAVIS

I HAD A DREAM

I WAS ALONE
IN THE MIDDLE OF A GALACTIC NIGHT
THE ENTIRE UNIVERSE WAS DARK
EXCEPT FOR A STRANGE EERIE NIGHT

WHY OH LIGHT
WHO YOU SHINE ON ME
DO YOU HAVE A PURPOSE
I CAN'T FATHOM NOR SEE

WHY IS THE DEPTHS OF THY FEELING
SO ETERNALLY DEEP
TO INVADE MY SANCTUARY
AWAKENING ME FROM A WELL NEEDED SLEEP

FROM WHERE IS YOUR ORIGIN
IS THERE NO WAY YOU CAN EXPLAIN
OR RELATE TO ME
BECAUSE OF MY EXTRATERRESTRIAL BRAIN

IS THE URGENCY THAT PRESSING
AS TO DISTURB THE AMBASSADOR OF FATE
WHICH TROUBLED BEING HAS SENT YOU
AND IS SO IMPETUOUS HE CAN NOT WAIT

SHOW YOUR BEFORE ME
UPON YOU LET MY EYES NOW GAZE
I GIVE YOU PERMISSION TO PRESENT YOURSELF
INSTEAD OF THIS LUMINOUS HAZE

AYE, TIS NONE OTHER BUT THEE
I SHOULD HAVE KNOWN ALL ALONG
WHY MUST YOU BE SO PERSISTENT
ARE YOU DENYING YOUR RIGHTFUL THRONE

I CAN'T CHANGE YOUR FATE
YOU ARE DESTINED TO DIE
THE ALMIGHTY HAS DECIDED THIS
EVEN I WOULD BE THROWN TO OBLIVION FOR
ASKING WHY

BUT IF YOU CAN RESTRAIN
YOUR EMPHATIC HOLLERING TO A SCREAM
YOUR LIFE LONG AMBITION I WILL SHOW YOU
WITH MY GUIDANCE IN YOUR DREAM

TELL THE WORLD IF YOU LIKE
EXPLAIN THE NIGHT IN WHICH YOUR DREAM
OCCURRED
SOME WILL BELIEVE YOU
AND OTHERS WILL NOT BELIEVE ONE SINGLE WORD

YEARS AHEAD IN WHICH YOU WILL NEVER SEE
WHEN THE GREATEST POET CAN'T MAKE ONE WORD
RHYME
AND OPPRESSED PEOPLE STILL STRIVE TO BE FREE
MARTIN LUTHER KING WILL REMEMBERED IN THE
ANNALS OF TIME

BUCK DAVIS

WRITTEN: NOVEMBER 1971

WRITINGS IN THE SAND

TO THE FAITHFUL
THOUGH THE STRAIT BE FEW
WALK WITH ME A WAYS
AS I WITNESS WITH YOU

BROTHERS AND SISTERS
LISTEN IF YOU HAVE EARS
MIRRORS ARE HYPNOTIZERS
WITH RERUNS OF CONFESSED FEARS

BEFORE THE MIRROR
FAITH DID ABOUND
IF THE PERSON WAS TRUE TO THEMSELVES
HIS OR HER PATH WAS EASILY FOUND

IT WAS THE FAITHLESS DOCTRINES
BRINGING NEW VOICES TO THE FORE
OFFERING AN ALTERNATIVE WITHOUT
CONDEMNATION
TO SEVER THE SEED'S CORE

IN THESE DOCTRINES FAITH WENT OUTWARD
INTO THE REALM OF AN ORDINARY MAN
TO GRASP THE ABUNDANCE OF NECESSITY
BECOMING ONE WITH THE LAND

STILL THE ONE WHO SET THE STARS
AND COMMANDED THE EARTH TO SPIN
WOULD NOT BE DENIED
BY A MIRROR REFLECTING THE WISHES OF MEN

THEREFORE CAME THE MIRROR OF FIRE
OF THINGS ONE OUGHT NOT TO DO
A SEAL UNTO THE WICKED
TO SPARE THE RIGHTEOUS FEW

DESTINIES BECAME SO ORDERED
HIS WILL BEING DONE
THE STAGE OF LIFE WAS SET
FOR THE FAITHFUL'S PROMISED ONE

YET HE THAT CAME FIRST
BY DEVOTION HE GAVE
THE FATHER OF FAITH
WENT TO HIS GRAVE

BY FAITH HE WALKED
WITH TESTIMONY OF HIS LIFE
BY OBEDIENCE HE WAS GIVEN GRACE
WHILE IN HIS HAND HE HELD A KNIFE

THE END OF LIFE IS NEARER
THAN MANY CARE TO THINK
FROM HERE TO ETERNITY CAN COME
AS FAST AS THE EYE CAN BLINK

THOSE WHO FOLLOW THE MIRROR'S PATH
GO WITH A CAUTIOUS SPEED
REMEMBERING THE CHOSEN
AND HE WHO PLANTED THEIR SEED

IN DARKNESS WITH POWER THOUGHTS
SECRECY BARS THE DOOR
DEMONS DEVISE DEVIOUSNESS
TO KEEP SOULS FAITHLESS AND POOR

FROM THE ORDER OF MELCHIZEDEK
  FAITH WAS REBORN
    CONFIRMED AND PRE-DESIGNED
      FROM ANCIENT PAGES TORN

AN ILLUMINATION OF LIGHT
  PIERCING THE INNER GLOOM
    PROJECTING AN ETERNAL MANSION
      WITH A LIGHTED UPPER ROOM

THE MASTER OF WONDERS
  THE QUICKENER OF THE MIND
    THE GATHERER OF THE SELECT
      UNITING ONE OF A KIND

AS IT WAS FORETOLD
  IT IS HAPPENING IN THIS VERY YEAR
    THE CORRUPTION IN THE MIRROR
      REINFORCED WITH CONSTANT FEAR

DOWNTOWN MIDTOWN SUBURB
  SCHOOL AND THE HOOD
    THE MIRROR HAS GONE TO TELEVISION
      WITH ACTORS FROM HOLLYWOOD

IT IS TIME TO REMEMBER
  THE WRITINGS IN THE SAND
    SILENCED ALL ACCUSERS
      BEFORE WHOM NONE COULD STAND

THE MIRROR HE COVERED
  IN A WELL TENDED MIND
    LIDS HE ALSO LIFTED
      FROM THOSE SPIRITUALLY BLIND

HE CAME NAKED AS ADAM AND EVE
 TO THE SEEING EYE
  SUFFERING THE MIRROR'S ATROCITIES
   SO THE FAITHFUL WOULD NEVER DIE

IN THESE DAYS AND TIMES
 THOUGHTS ARE MAGNIFIED BY THE ELECTODE
 SENDER
  THEY ARE DESIGNED TO EMBRACE ALL
   THE FAITHFUL AND THE PRETENDER

SO LISTEN CAREFULLY WITH INNER EYES AND
EARS
 AND NOT A LUSTFUL WHIM
  AS YOU MIND THE MIRROR
   BY STAYING INSIDE OF HIM

TO ANY DESIRING GRACE
 HERE IS A MOST SACRED CLUE
  WITH FAITH REACH UP
   TO TOUCH THE LATCHET OF HIS SHOE

                              BUCK DAVIS

TIMES

IN THE BEST OF TIMES
WE NEED A FRIEND
IN THE WORST OF TIMES
THE NEED HAS NO END

IT IS HARD WHEN TIMES ARE GOOD
TO REMAIN TRUE
DIVERSITIES OF MATERIALISTIC
MANIPULATIONS
OFFERS A THOUSAND ALTERNATIVES TO DO

SO WE DRAW A LINE
TO KEEP OUR PATH STRAIGHT
HOLD ON TO ETHICAL REASONING
TO LOCK OR UNLOCK OUR EMOTIONAL STATE

FRIENDS BECOMES BAROMETERS
THEY KNOW AS SOON AS WE MEET
TO ADDRESS US TO OUR COLDNESS
OR STRIP TO OUR HEAT

THUS INTERACTION IS ACCORDED
ON A EQUALIBRICATED SCALE
A DETERMINANT OF A SUCCESSFUL
RELATIONSHIP
OR ONE DOOMED TO FAIL

IT IS NEAR IMPOSSIBLE IN THE WORST OF
TIMES
TO BE TRUE EVEN TO YOURSELF
WITH SO MANY THINGS NEEDING TO BE DONE
IMMEDIATELY
ONLY TO BE LAID ON THE SHELF

THE AUTOMATED FUNCTIONING OF OUR
THOUGHT PROCESSES
SOMETIMES BECOME TOO MUCH
DEPRIVED OF EARTHLY COMFORTS
DEPRIVED OF A LOVING TOUCH

WANTING TO GIVE OF YOURSELF
THAT WHICH MAKES YOU GAIN
LOCKED IN THE TURMOIL OF THE TIMES
CONSUMED WITH THE BURNING PAIN

APOLOGETIC FOR ANY OFFENSES
TO ONE HELD DEAR
PROMISING FUTURISTIC REWARDS
ONCE THE WRONG IS BROUGHT TO BEAR

WE CAN ONLY HOPE THAT DISCERNMENT OF
INAPPROPRIATENESS
WILL HEAL THAT WHICH WAS BROKE
AND TWO HEARTS WILL BEAT AS ONE
WITH EVERY MOMENTOUS STROKE

THE DAWN OF DIALECTICS

CAPITALISM SOCIALISM COMMUNISM
ALL THREE ARE ON THE SAME COURSE
USING PERSUASION MANIPULATION COERCION
OR FINALLY ALL OUT FORCE

LET US JOURNEY BACKWARDS
TO A TIME OF LONG AGO
TO THE DIALECTICS OF SOCRATES
ARGUING THINGS YOU THINK YOU ALREADY KNOW

YOU SEE THE GRANDEUR OF LIFE'S EXPECTATION
ISN'T REALLY THERE
WE LIVE WITHIN CONCENTRIC CIRCLES OF LAWS
THE GENERAL PUBLIC HAS TO BEAR

PLATO ARGUED FOR HIS ELITES
THOSE FEW DESTINED TO RULE
ASSUMING THE POLIS WOULD FOLLOW
HE LAID THE PRINCIPLES OF HIS PLUTONIAN SCHOOL

BUT WHERE THERE IS NO SENSE OF DUTY
THERE IS NO REASON TO OBEY
THE POLIS BELONGS TO THE PEOPLE
WHO VOTES THEIR FINAL SAY

IN THE THEORY OF OPPOSITES
ARISTOTLE WOULD SURELY AGREE
THE INSTANT A LIE ARRIVES
THE TRUTH IS SET FREE

TO FIND TRUTHS
ENTAILS A TIRELESS QUEST
THE POINT WHERE THE SEARCH BEGINS
IN NEAR MAN'S BEST

NICOLAI MACHIAVELLIAN'S ADVISE TO RULERS
CONCERNING THE PRINCE OF WAR AND THE PRINCE
OF PEACE
DID NOT DEAL WITH NUCLEAR DISCUSSIONS
OF A HALF-MAN AND A HALF-BEAST

IS THERE A BEAST BEHIND PERSONA
HOLDING OUR LIVES IN A NUCLEAR SPHERE
LET US HOPE HIS DESIRES ARE WELL FED
OR POOF – THE WHOLE WORLD COULD DISAPPEAR

KARL MARX ONCE SAID
IN A VERY MOMENTOUS BREATH
THAT THE ROOT OF MAN
IS MAN HIMSELF

THAT THE FREEDOM IN MAN'S NATURE
DOESN'T DEPEND UPON AN EXTERNAL THING
BUT THAT IT ROCKS ON THE OCEAN OF ETERNAL
KNOWLEDGE
TO THE TUNE HIS EMOTIONS SING

CHAIRMAN MAO TZE TUNG PRACTICED
CONTRADICTIONS
OPPOSITION AD INFINITUM
ANTAGONISTIC VS. ANTI-ANTAGONISTIC
UNTIL THE SYNTHESIS BECOMES THE SUM

MEANING IF AT FIRST YOU DON'T SUCCEED
YOU TRY AND TRY AGAIN
YOUR THEORY VS. YOUR METHOD
TO ACHIEVE YOUR OWN DESIRED END

PICTURE THOMAS HOBBES
OR THE THEORY HE SAW
WHERE THE GREATEST LIBERTY OF SUBJECTS
DEPENDETH UPON SILENCE OF THE LAW

IN THIS THEORY EVERY MAN
WOULD BE HIS OWN FINAL JUDGE
I WONDER ON MATTERS OF ECONOMIC INTEREST
WOULD EITHER OPPOSITE DARE TO BUDGE

JOHN LOCKE PLACES MAN IN A STATE OF NATURE
OR A CONSTITUTIONAL SOCIETY
GOVERNED BY RATIONAL LAWS
WILLED BY A SUPREME DEITY

LOCKE'S PROPOSAL FOR JUSTICE
SEEMS ADEQUATE AND GRAND
TO BE WILLED BY A DEITY
AND EXECUTED BY A PIOUS MAN

THOMAS JEFFERSON CHANGED LIFE LIBERTY AND
PROPERTY
TO PRECARIOUSLY READ
LIFE LIBERTY AND THE PURSUIT OF HAPPINESS
AS OPTIONS LOYAL CITIZENS NEED

I NEED A THOUSAND ACRES
AS MY CONSTITUTIONAL PROPERTY
HE COULD'VE KEPT HIS PURSUIT OF HAPPINESS
THAT DEALT ME MY ANCESTORS SLAVISH POVERTY

Buck Davis

JACQUES ROUSSEAU ARGUING FOR FREEDOMS
SAYS NO MAN CAN BE ENSLAVED WITHOUT HIS OWN
CONSENT
AND TO WASTE IT AT A WEAK MOMENT
ONLY ILLUSTRATES HOW CHEAPLY IT CAN BE SPENT

IS YOUR REPRESENTATIVE EXPRESSING THE
GENERAL WILL
OR THE WILL OF ALL
VOTING HIS CONSTITUENTS WISHES
OR DEALS MADE IN THE HALL

LET US EXAMINE HIS WORDS
VOTE FOR ME
A MAN FOR THE PEOPLE
AND I WILL SET YOU FREE

IF SOMEONE NEEDS FREEING
THIS IMPLIES HE IS ALREADY CAUGHT
SO WHY RESELL SOMETHING
EVERYONE HAS ALREADY BOUGHT

DIALECTICS IS A TWO-EDGED SWORD
THAT CUTS BOTH WAYS
THE HOLY MEN IN TEMPLES
THE CAPITALIST THAT SPENDS AND PLAYS

WHO IS THERE AMONG US THAT OPPOSES
CONSTITUTIONS
TO WHAT EXTENT TO WHAT DEGREES
REMEMBERING WE CONSTANTLY WATCH TELEVISION
VIEWING THE TALLEST OF TREES

AS MARTIN LUTHER KING SAID OURS IS PERFECT
IF FOLLOWED TO THE LETTER
SO WHAT WE NEED IS A TELEOLOGICAL DESIGN
TO MAKE THE HEARTS OF MEN BETTER

FOR MARTIN TOUCHED THE GOD FIGURE
THAT IS INHERENT IN EVERYONE
AND BECAUSE OF HIS PROPHETIC NATURE
HE WAS TAKEN FROM US BEFORE HIS WORK WAS
DONE

THE FORCES HE OPPOSED
LINGER TO THIS DAY
USING NEW METHODS OF MODUS OPERANDI
SEPARATING YOU FROM YOUR WEEKLY PAY

HIS DREAM IS ALREADY FLEETING
AND WE ALL KNOW WHY
FOR UNLIKE MARTIN OUR LEADERS OF TODAY
ARE NOT WILLING TO DIE

TO STEP OUT ON THE STAGE OF LIFE
AN ATTEMPT TO HARNESS THE FORCES OF THE WIND
WILL BRING YOU MARTYRDOM FOR SURE
BUT ALSO A SOLITARY JOURNEY WITHOUT A CLOSE
FRIEND

MARTIN WIELDED THE SWORD OF DIALECTICS
HE SHOWED THE WORLD WHITE AMERICA'S TRUE
FACE
HE TAUGHT PEACE AND PACIFISM
SUFFERING THEIR VIOLENCE DIRECTED AT THE
BLACK RACE

THE CONVERSATION CONTINUES CONCERNING CIVIL
RIGHTS
RIGHT DOWN TO THIS VERY AGE
ALLOWING REFERENCES AND CONTRADICTIONS
AS UNDERSTOOD BY EACH UP AND COMING SAGE

ACHIEVEMENT OF THE HIGHEST GOOD
IS WHERE WE ARE TOLD TO AIM
WALKING BACKWARDS INTO THE FUTURE
GUIDED ONLY BY THE PATH WE CAME

BUCK DAVIS

THE SCALES UNTO HUMANITY

BLUE SKIES FAIR WEATHER
 HERALDS A PROMISING DAY
  HORIZONS ARE LIFTED TO THE HEAVENS
   AS OUR IMAGINATIONS DANCE AND PLAY

WITHIN THE OUTLINED BOUNDARIES
 OF A SANE MIND
  WE EXPLORE SHRINKING REALITIES
   WHICH ARE GETTING HARDER TO FIND

CONFINED TO A BED
 OUR ONLY MOVEMENT IS THOUGHT
  OUR ONLY VEHICLE POSSIBLE
   ARE THE LIFE LESSONS WE HAVE BEEN TAUGHT

DEPENDENT UPON OTHERS
 FOR EVERY LITTLE THING
  ALL WE CAN GIVE IN RETURN
   IS THE SPECIAL LOVE WE PERSONALLY BRING

A PLEASANT GREETING
 A WARM TOUCHING SMILE
  A SINCERE COMPLIMENT
   DELIVERED WITH THE INNOCENCE OF A CHILD

PROUDLY DISPLAYING THE WILL TO GO ON
 IN SPITE OF INFINITIES AND ALL
  TO HUMBLE TO BEG
   USUALLY TO WEAK TO CALL

TEACHING OTHERS TO BE THANKFUL
 THE LITTLE THINGS DO NOT CURSE
  FOR EVEN WE ARE BLESSED
   LOOK AROUND THERE ARE OTHERS MUCH WORSE

WE WORK THE PROFESSIONALS AND LOVED ONES
  UNTIL THEY TIRE AND SLIP AWAY
    DURING THESE TIMES OF WAKEFUL SOLITUDE
    MOSTLY WE PRAY

SOME OF US PRAY FOR MORE LIFE
  SOME OF US PRAY FOR A QUICK DEATH
    MOSTLY WE ALL PRAY FOR OUR HELPERS
    THANKING GOD IN EVERY BREATH

ONE MILLION WHY ME'S
  HAVE NOT DIVULGED GOD'S ULTIMATE PLAN
    I THINK IT IS TO MEASURE HUMANKIND'S HUMANITY
    IN DIRECT RELATION TO DIFFERENT NEEDS OF HIS FELLOW MAN

FOR WE WHO ARE PARALYZED WITNESS TO GOD AND OURSELVES
  EVERY SINGLE DAY WE LIVE
    BLESSING AND PRAISING THOSE WHO HELP US
    WITH ALL THE LOVE WE HAVE TO GIVE.

                    BUCK DAVIS

LET US LOOK AT THE SYSTEM

THE MOVEMENT OF THE WORLD
AS IT IS TODAY
IS A MIRROR FACING A MIRROR
CAPITALIZATION TURNING THIS AND THAT WAY

THE <u>RICH</u> GET RICHER
THAN THEY HAVE EVER BEEN
SECURED AND UNHARMED
BY THE WAGES OF SIN

THE <u>POOR</u> GET POORER
THAN THEY HAVE A RIGHT TO BE
SECURED AND ENHANCED
BY NO FREEDOM AND NO LIBERTY

THE <u>PREACHERS</u> ARE STILL PREACHING
ON ETERNITIES OF HEAVEN AND HELL
FAULTLESS OF THEIR FLOCK'S AMBITION
PRAISING RATIONALIZATIONS THEY TELL

THE <u>PEOPLE</u> ARE WAVERING
BETWEEN RIGHT AND WRONG
LISTENING TO DIVERSE POLITICAL LEADERS
DANCING IN UNITY TO THE SAME SONG

<u>DOCTORS</u> SWORN TO AN OATH
ARE TURNING SICK PEOPLE AWAY
BECAUSE THE SYSTEM KEEP THEM SO POOR
BETWEEN MEALS THEY CAN'T AFFORD TO PAY

<u>LAWYERS</u> ARE DOING A LANDSLIDE BUSINESS
LAUGHING ALL THE WAY TO THE BANK
AS THEY STEAL FROM LEGAL ILLITERATES
CITIZENS TOO NUMB TO THINK

Buck Davis

THE <u>POLICE</u> ARE BEING TRAINED
TO CREATE CRIME IF NONE EXIST
AND DRIVE HOME FEAR TWENTY FOUR SEVEN
WITH AN IRON FIST

WALL STREET IS STILL THE ODDS MAKER
THE BIG BOY TO BE BEATEN
BUT LIKE MOST MIDDLE AMERICAN INVESTORS
ALL AMERICA IS BEING EATEN

THE PRESIDENT IS STILL STUTTERING
AND STUMBLING ALONG
LIKE NERO WHEN ROME BURNED
PLAYING THE SAME SONG

THE CHILDREN ARE BEING PUNISHED
NOT GETTING THE PROPER DIET TO EAT
THE PROPER HOME OR EDUCATION
ALL AROUND THEY ARE GETTING BEAT

THE AGED ARE DISCARDED
SLAMMED INTO AN ANTISEPTIC HOME
THERE TO SPEND THEIR GOLDEN YEARS
ARRESTED, ARTHRITIC AND ALONE

A KILLER CALLED AIDS IS RAMPANT
THE COUNTRY SEEMS NOT TO MIND
UNTIL IT REACHES THEIR HOME
AND TOUCHES THEIR OWN KIND

PRISONS ARE BEING BUILT
AT AN EVER INCREASING PACE
PRISONERS RUNNING THROUGH THE COURTS
ARE CURRENTLY WINNING THE RACE

THE WORKPLACE IS BECOMING DE-UNIONIZED
WITH ALL DUE SPEED
PEOPLE CAN'T FIND WORK
ALL BECAUSE OF GREED

THE EDUCATORS ARE QUIET
WHEN NOT IN SCHOOL
THEY HAVE A SECURE JOB
WHY PLAY THE PART OF A FOOL

THE MINIMUM WAGE LAW
IS A CRUEL JOKE
PASSED BY THE CORPORATE LOBBYIST
TO SUPPRESS POOR FOLK

THIS IS THE WAY OF THE WORLD
FOR BETTER OR WORSE
FOR THE ONES WHO ARE LAST
FOR THE ONES WHO ARE FIRST

DO PEOPLE ACTUALLY BELIEVE
THIS WAS THE WAY THE WORLD WAS TO BE
I MEAN IT IS SO OBVIOUSLY PLAIN
IT IS SO SOMETHING A BLIND MAN CAN SEE

BUCK DAVIS

MENTAL MADNESS

TODAY WAS NOT
  TOMORROW IS NEVER HERE
    YESTERDAY IS ONLY A DREAM
      OCCURRING ONCE A YEAR

BUT WHO AM I
  KNOWING I CAN'T TRUTHFULLY SAY
    BEING TOWED THROUGH THE CURRENTS OF TIME
      WITH MYSELF TO PORTRAY

AND WHAT AM I
  FLESH AND BONE
    VAIN IN THOUGHT
      A LIGHT NEVER TO HAVE SHONE

DISGUISED IN GARMENTS
  HIDING EMOTIONAL DESIRE
    TO LIVE INSIDE OF SANITY
      OR GRIEVE THE PASSING OF SOLAR FIRE

DAY HAS BECOME NIGHT
  LIGHT AND DARK ARE THE SAME
    LUNCH IS HOURLY
      BECAUSE CORTISANS HAS NO SHAME

WE ALL ARE INDENTURED
  FREELY BEING BOUGHT AND SOLD
    WE BELONG TO FORD, CHEVROLET AND CHARMIN
      OR OTHER CORPORATE NAMES WE HAVEN'T BEEN
      TOLD

RUNNING, JUMPING, CLIMBING CLAWING
  REALLY REACHING NO-WHERE
    CURSING, BEGGING, SWEARING, CRYING
      TRYING TO TAKE THE NEXT FELLOW'S SHARE

WALKING IN CIRCLES
  A HIGHLY INTELLIGENT BRAIN
    ARGUMENTATIVE AND LOOSE-LIPPED
      GOOSE-STEPPING THROUGH THE DRY RAIN

HAIL TO THE FLESH
  AH..AH WHAT IS HIS NAME
    IT DOES NOT MATTER
      POLITICIANS PLAY THE SAME POLITICAL GAME

THERE REMAINS TOO MUCH NOISE IN SILENCE
  AND DEATHLY QUIET IN A CROWD
    TOO SICK IN THE FACTORIES
      TO PRETEND TO BE PATRIOTIC AND PROUD

I GUESS I HAVE TO KEEP SEARCHING
  PLACING MY DREAMS UPON A DISTANT STAR
    KNOWING AT MIDNIGHT TOMORROW WILL REMAIN
    TWENTY FOUR HOURS TO FAR.

BUCK DAVIS

SISTER EVIL

Sister Evil
  A tempting beautiful witch
   A no-good Whore
    A two-timing Bitch

The Empress of murder
  The Mother of crime
   The wife of the wicked
    The Lover of old man Time

Darker than Doom's Dimension
  Atrocious as Satan's Den
   Hideous as Medusa's Hair
    With the strength of ten thousand men

Higher than eyes can see
  Wider than measurements can take
   Longer than existence exist
    Eruptive as a volcanic earthquake

Sister evil
  The inventor of unscrupulous lies
   To the thousands who seek supposed joys
    While laying between her thighs

She smiles
  While her eyes stab her victim through
   You are forever trapped in her web
    And there is not a damn thing one can do

You can't go back
  You can't go ahead
   You are no longer a part of the living
    After you and Sister Evil are wed

WARRIOR'S LOVE

Unto these eyes of mine
Without reminisce of love before
All women created so divine
Now an unbelievable vision stands in my door

From whence she came
Only my subconscious know
An assassin of the heart
And lovingly so

Why has she chosen me
To taste the nectar of her breast
Knowing me for what I am
Knowing that I would kill for less

Why has she brought to me
That which is too previous to give
That which I can never fully return
Try as I must as long as I may live

Woman your beauty taunts me
To want you more
Your love is beckoning for my soul
Reaching through the iron door

I am a warrior
For years I have stood and heard your moans
With steel in my hands
And ice in my bones

Wanting to feel your body
Pressing you near
Calming your sensuality
Stilling your fear

Your beauty is unquestionable
Your love so sweet and kind
A rich pure sensation
At times it controls my mind

Now if I had said this years ago
Would it have made a difference then
Or would you have preferred being called
A dear friend

You see this was my dilemma
An answer I could not take
I would ask now
But I fear that it might be a mistake

To realize no one cares
That I am truly all alone
That even my dream
Has faded and gone

For I am too vulnerable
To envision a Lady
Who does not know her own heart
And acts kind of shady

For in my realm
There is only black and white
You are either dead wrong
Or rich and absolutely right

Only the strong survive
The good they die young
Their memories vanish in time
Also the songs they sung

If I were not a warrior
You would not wait there
If I were not a survivor
There would be no need to care

I am holding my peace
Walking a path not very wide
I do it conditionally
To one day walk by your side

Looking at this image of you
All my ghosts begin to slowly fade
Your loveliness is only overshadowed
By the tears that you have paid

Cling to my writings
Linger on every line
Compare me to all the others
See if you can say you are not mine

Not too possess
Surely not to own
But to love every inch of you
Down to the marrow of your bone

Princess where are the dragons
That I must slay
I will see you freed of encumbrances
Or die this very day

And after that statement the vision
Vanished and was no more
Leaving me here stranded and alone
Wrestling dragons to reach your door

BUCK DAVIS

Buck Davis

GYPSY WOMAN

IN A ROOM THICK WITH CROWD
VIOLIN MUSIC DANCED ACROSS THE AIR
HER FRAGRANCES CREATED A MELODY
AROMATIC FLAVORS WITH A FLAIR

BEAUTIFUL AS A BABY BIRD
IN IT'S FIRST FLIGHT
A STARRY EYED CREATURE
QUEEN OF THE NIGHT

OUR EYES MET SLOWLY
LIGHTENING BOLTS TOOK HOLD
SHE LOOKED FROM ACROSS THE ROOM
WITH EYES FLASHING AND BOLD

I WAS ROOTED TO MY SPOT
AS SHE DROPPED A NUMBERED NOTE AT MY FEET
GAVE ME A MONA LISA'S SMILE
HALF WICKED HALF SWEET

FROM THAT MOMENT ON
I WAS HER MAN
BEGUILED BY HER BEAUTY
LOVING IN A TROUBLED LAND

WE MET SECRETLY
STEALING AWAY WHETHER WRONG OR RIGHT
TO FERMENT NATURE'S JUICES
AS VIOLENTLY AS ANY FIGHT

HOW WILD AND CAPTIVATING
THE TYPE OF LOVE SHE GAVE
LEAVING BITE MARKS AND SCRATCHES
TO STAY TILL THE GRAVE

SHE STOLE HERSELF
INTO THE BEST OF ME
A DAMSEL IN DISTRESS
SENT ME TO MY KNEE

SHE CAME AND WENT
LIKE A THIEF ON THE RUN
HER COMING BROUGHT HAPPINESS
HER GOING HEAVY AS A TON

SHE NEEDED ME ONCE
HOW BADLY I DID NOT KNOW
I WAS INTO THE AFFAIRS OF THE WORLD
MAKING MY BEST THROW

FOR A SHORT WHILE
WE LIVED TO BE IN EACH OTHER'S MIND
BEFORE MY LIFESTYLE RAN HER AWAY
BACK TO HER OWN KIND

NOW SHE INVADES MY DREAMS
LIKE A HUNTER SEEKING GAME
SUMMONING ME TO STAND BEFORE HER
CHAINED AND TAME

IN LOVING RETROSPECT
HER MEMORY IS AN INSTANT REPLAY
AS I DREAM OF MY TOMORROWS
LIVING IN THOUGHTS OF YESTERDAY

BUCK DAVIS

(WRITTEN ESPECIALLY FOR A FRIEND, NICK, WHO
STILL CARES FOR HIS GYPSY WOMAN)

SEVEN TIERS TO JOURNEY'S END

A Chaldean Princess
  Seemingly chiseled from stone
    Recreating a beauty spoken of
      In a time long gone

I bow before your feet
  In your presence glad only to exist
    A mortal prisoner to your whims
      Your beauty I can't resist

Your milky long hair
  Your invitingly soft eyes
    Your flaunting of femininity
      Your hot passionate lies

Those few lines were anchors
  Dropped in the tenderest section of your heart
    Where I am about to journey
      I wanted you to know before I start

On the First Tier is Humiliation
  For not being wed
    Imagining unspoken conversations
      About something someone might have said

Woman your heart should not be a mirror
  Reflecting opinions argued in the world
    Do not make It a crossword puzzle
      It should be virgin as a little girl

On the Second Tier is Sharing
  You give and nothing is what you get
    It shows you are a poor gambler
      And really you should not bet

You roll the dice of emotions
　As you throw yourself into the pelting rain
　　Riding the currents of expectations
　　　Leaving a residue of unclaimed pain

On the Third Tier is Confusion
　So much fear and doubt
　　Like a bird in an open cage
　　　Afraid to climb the air and fly out

Faith should not start from the world
　But from within
　　Attuned to your natural inclinations
　　　Away from the lustful stares of base men

On the Fourth Tier is Dependency
　The inability to stand as one
　　Pulled by the gravity of a moon
　　　Encircled by yet another sun

It takes a quiet strong spirit
　To live in disobedience of the few
　　Travel a singular path in life
　　　Keeping your direction straight and true

On the Fifth Tier is Defense
　Delivered with disarming tears
　　Expounding your endless virtues
　　　Redefining your day to day fears

Sorrow is habitual to some
　Now Joy is the feeling to know
　　It's walls are too high for short legs
　　　Whereas Sorrow's intention is hitting sort of low

On the Sixth Tier is Remembrances
  Of a love long lost
    A lasting impression of near perfection
      Paid for it an awful cost

Seeking reduplication in every near face
  Like watching a movie without an end
    Remembrances should be stored as treasures
      Not as an instrument to judge other men

The Seventh Tier is the Center of You
  It is to beautiful...in here to Believe
    No canvas could hold your illumination
      Duplication a brush could never achieve

I am here inside of You
  As no one ever before
    I came of my own free will
      After you opened the door

Will you ask me to leave
  Or will I be forced to stay
    I am in your heart
      You have the final say

The Happiness you now feel
  Is beginning to grow
    It releases a sweet fragrance
      Promising secrets only I will know

Understand Chaldean Princess
  The feelings developing between you and me
    Is not on the plane of illusions
      It is in your heart where it should be

Hidden from informative eyes
  Hidden from gossiping ears
    A haven and a sanctity
      To visit often during the coming years

Your Love has cut my anchor line
  I am marooned and can not roam
    This then is my Eternal resting place
      Your heart is now my happy home

If after reading these descencions you do not know me
  Then sadly beautiful one I do not know you
    Then this journey was all make believe
      And not one word of it was true

So where I am could be Heaven
  Or it could be a lonely Hell
    As I stand on the threshold of your thoughts
      Looking for signs only time will tell

Buck Davis

LOVE'S BYPLAY

EVERYONE IS A STUDENT UNTO LOVE
FROM SOMEONE ESPECIALLY DEAR
COMFORTED IN THEIR PRESENCE
WITH THE ADDED ASSURANCES OF BEING NEAR

WE ALL SEEK SOME SORT OF LOVING TREASURE
BUT FEW SELDOM FIND
STUMBLING ALONG LIKE DRUNKARDS
VIRTUALLY BLIND

FOR THE REASONS OF CAUSE AND EFFECT
WE ARE CHAINED TO OUR INTENT
REALIZING WE HAVE WHAT WE WANTED
AND NOT GETTING WHAT WE MEANT

SO WE THROW AWAY FEELINGS
WITHOUT SOCIETAL SHAME
MEET BACK IN THE MAINSTREAM
TO REPLAY LOVE'S GAME

A MOMENT HERE
A SMILE THERE
A TOUCH BEFORE DEPARTURE
DRIFTING LIKE A FRAGRANCE IN THE AIR

WAS IT HER HAIR
WAS IT HER EYES
WAS IT HER KISSES
WAS IT HER PASSIONATE LIES

WAS IT HER CHANGING MOODS
WAS IT HER SEDUCTIVE WALK
WAS IT HER SOFT BODY
WAS IT HER NASTY TALK

I DON'T REALLY KNOW
I CAN'T TRUTHFULLY SAY
IT COULD HAVE NONE OR ALL OF THOSE QUALITIES
YET I AM A WINNER IN LOVE'S BYPLAY

IT COULD HAVE BEEN HER NEARNESS
IT COULD HAVE BEEN HER TOUCH
THINGS I NEEDED IN MY LIFE
AND GREW TO LOVE VERY MUCH

IF I COULD DO ANY BETTER
I CAN'T SEE HOW
SO TO ALL SEEKERS YOU HAVE MY BLESSINGS
IT IS TIME I TOOK MY FINAL BOW

I AM STUNG WITH JOY
BEING CARESSED BY THE WIND
GATHERED INTO HER BOSOM
MY WOMAN, LOVER, AND CONSUMMATE FRIEND

BUCK DAVIS

INTREPID DISCLOSURES

BETWEEN THE LAYERS OF ILLUSIONS
 SIDE-STEPPING VALUES STANDARDS AND ALL
  ADORNED WITH RAVENOUS BEAUTY
   A WOMAN ANSWERING NATURE'S CALL

POSSESSING FEMININITY BEYOND COMPARISON
 BARING YOUR BREAST WITH A SMILE
  CREATING A SCENE TO INCITE UNDULATION
   REPRODUCING A FAMILIAR STYLE

CLOTHED IN SILKY UNDER THINGS
 BARELY COVERING YOUR MILKY SKIN
  PRACTICING THE FINE ART OF SEDUCTION
   CAPTURING THE LUSTFUL IMAGINATION OF MEN

A VERY SOULFUL WOMAN
 A PRINCESS IN YOUR OWN RIGHT
  OFFERING YOUR SELF TO THE EVENING
   THROWING YOURSELF INTO THE NIGHT

POLITELY EXTRICATING YOUR FEELING
 FROM MEN PROVEN TO BE TAME
  CURSING THEIR NEAR IMPOTENCE
   FOR NOT BEING ABLE TO FINISH THE GAME

STALKING THE HAUNTED STREETS
 SEARCHING TAVERN AND BARS
  LOOKING FOR FADING MEMORIES
   HOPING TO HEAL OPEN SCARS

GIVING YOURSELF TO MINDLESS MINIONS
 WHEN FINISHED GO THEIR SEPARATE WAY
  BOASTING OF SPENT PASSIONS
   LIKE LITTLE BOYS AT SCHOOLYARD PLAY

LEAVING YOU OBNOXIOUS AND BEWILDERED
  CHASTISING YOURSELF WITH UNBELIEF
    RETURNING TO THE MIRROR WITH POWDER AND
    ROUGE
      TO PRESENT AN IMAGE OF SATISFACTION AND
      RELIEF

UNDERSTAND ME PRECIOUS ONE
  IT IS WAY PAST TIME YOU WERE TOLD
    THESE SCENES MEANT FOR PROCREATION
      ARE THOUSANDS OF YEARS OLD

THE CHANCE GAMES OF ARDOR SELECTION
  THE ORIGINAL RULES ARE NOT BEING KEPT
    WHO CAN TELL WHOM FOR SURE
      WHEREWITHAL THEY HAVE SLEPT

THE PURPOSE OF DRINKING WATER
  IS TO QUENCH YOUR THIRST
    IF INTIMACY IN COITAL EMBRACE MEANS
    SOMETHING
      NEITHER WILL REACH THEIR SUMMIT FIRST

IT DOES NOT PAY TO BE WITH SOMEONE
  SIMPLY TO AVOID BEING ALONE
    THE VARIETAL GHOSTS OF SOLITUDE WILL RETURN
    MINUTES AFTER THEY ARE GONE

THE WORLD IS YOUR PLAYGROUND
  MATURITY IS A FLUORESCENCE LIGHT
    THE VINTAGE OF INTOXICANTS WILL TAKE THEIR
    TOLL
      FROM PROMISCUOUS LADIES RUMMAGING
    THROUGH THE NIGHT

IT IS TIME TO EULOGIZE THE PAST
  TOMORROW BEGIN FRESH AND ANEW
    DO NOT EPITOMIZE THE HARLOT OF TINSEL TOWN
      LET OTHERS EMULATE THE BEAUTY IN YOU

WHY STOOP TO DEGRADATION OF YOURSELF
  TO ACHIEVE A SEXUAL AIM
    MATURATION HAS ONLY TO APPEAR BEFORE
    SEEING EYES
      TO ACHIEVE INSTANT HARMONY AND FAME

SWEET PASSIONATE LUSCIOUS MOONCHILD
  HOLD YOUR REASONING CAPABILITIES UP HIGH
    PRETENSES OF IGNORANCE WILL NOT PRODUCE
    LOVE
      REPUDIATE THIS SELF-WILLED LIE

I HAVE TORN AWAY YOUR BEWITCHING MASK
  BEFORE ME YOU ARE AS NAKED AS YOU ENTERED
  THE WORLD
    THE PURPOSE OF THESE INTREPID DISCLOSURES
      IS TO LEVITATE A WOMAN FROM A GIRL

IF A ONE NIGHT STAND IS ALL YOU WANT
  THEN THE LOVE IN YOUR HEART HAS ESCAPED
    IF THE FUTURE IS PROMISED AND YOU DON'T GET IT
      THEN SUGAR YOU ARE BEING RAPED

WHO AM I YOU SAY
  I AM A MAN OF HARD YEARS
    SPEAKING FROM A WEALTH OF EXPERIENCES
      SEEN THROUGH EYES THAT HAS WEPT DRY TEARS

I AM A BIG GAME HUNTER
  ANNOUNCING YOUR HUNTING DAYS ARE GONE
    I HAVE SEARCHED SIX CONTINENTS WIDE
      TO FIND YOU AND BAG YOU AS MY OWN

UNLIKE TYPICAL HUNTERS
  I POACHED HEAVILY UPON THE LAWS OF MAN
    IMPRISONED FROM MY OBVIOUS TRANSGRESSIONS
      ONLY MY SPIRIT IS FREE TO ROAM THE LAND

AFTER YEARS OF RECONCILIATORY REPARATIONS
  MY THIRD EYE DID RETURN AND UNFOLD
    SO EVEN AFTER HEAVENLY FORGIVENESS
      MANKIND IS STILL EXACTING THEIR VENGEFUL
      TOLL

A PICTURE BEARING AN IMAGE OF YOU
  REOPENED MY MIND'S DOOR
    A WOMAN HIDING BEHIND HYPOCRISY
      SHELTERING YOUR WOUNDED HEART'S CORE

IT IS AS BEAUTIFUL AS A BABY DOE
  ON SPINDLY LEGS
    HUMBLE AS A HOMELESS PERSON
      THAT CRIES AND BEGS

AS LOVING AS AN ATTENTIVE MOTHER
  TO HER NEW BORN CHILD
    CONSTANT AS A CLOCK
      TICKING ALL THE WHILE

DEDICATED AS A DOCTOR
  WANTING TO CURE THE WORLD
    THE SALT OF THE EARTH
      A TRUE ONE MAN'S GIRL

ENCHANTING AS AN EMPRESS
  WIELDING THE POWERS OF HER MAN
    INDUSTRIOUS AS A QUEEN BEE
      PRODUCING ALL SHE CAN

WHO CAN RESIST YOUR FEMININE CHARMS
  WHEN YOU MOAN SENSUAL SIGHS
    MASSAGE YOUR SENSITIVE NIPPLES
      DISPLAY THE BASE OF YOUR VELVETY THIGHS

WHO CAN ENTERTAIN A SANE THOUGHT
  ENTERING YOUR SOFT MAIDENHEAD
    TRAVERSE YOUR CANAL'S COURSE
      WHERE MANY DESIRED BUT FEW HAVE TREAD

WHO CAN DOWNSHIFT STAMINA
  WHEN YOU ARE PUMPING STRONG
    VERY MUCH INTO YOUR ELEMENT
      ANSWERING THE TUNE OF NATURE'S SONG

WHO COULD NOT CARESS YOUR TREMBLING BODY
  AFTERWARDS PRESSING YOU NEAR
    AS YOUR TREMORS SLOWLY SUBSIDE
      KISS YOU TENDERLY AND DEAR

MY LONG WANDERING MOONCHILD
  I HAVE TASTED YOUR DELICIOUS NATURE'S BREW
    DRANK DEEPLY FROM YOUR POINTED BREASTS
      MADE JUNGLE LOVE ALL NIGHT TO YOU

TRY TO REMEMBER ALL THE TIMES
  YOU WENT HUNTING IN YOUR BED
    IT WASN'T ME PENETRATING YOUR BODY
      I WAS THE EXOTIC WISH IN YOUR HEAD

THERE WHERE TIMES YOU EXPERIENCED ORGASMS
OTHER TIMES YOUR JUICES WOULD NOT FLOW
WEARY OF YOUR SELF-DELUSIONARY ANTICS
I SPELLED MY DISSATISFACTION N..O..

YOU KNOW WHAT I AM SAYING IS TRUE
TO PROVE IT I WILL WAGER YOU A BET
CHECK YOUR PANTIES RIGHT NOW
TELL ME-ARE YOU WET

THESE INTREPID DISCLOSURES
IF READ MORE THAN TWICE YOU WILL FIND
I WILL REMAIN FOREVER WITHIN THE BARRIERS
YOU CONSTRUCTED IN YOUR MIND

BUCK DAVIS

THE RIDER OF THE DARK HORSE
CALLED MIDNIGHT

I am riding poised
  As trouble passes me by
    Munching on frozen hopes
      Distilled from a hopeful eye

My time has not come
  It is yet to be born
    As I float in the currents of diversity
      Bloodied battered and torn

As a gambler my fate has been dealt
  Another losing hand
    Like any other high stakes gambler
      I am playing it the best I can

It is needless to say
  I alone am solely to blame
    I chose to ride the dark horse
      Midnight is his name

I rode him to war
  Death marked our trail
    Claiming the fallen bodies
      Those doomed to fail

I rode him home
  No peace did we find
    Only a different war
      With battles none to kind

Midnight roared back on his haunches
  And away we did go
    Over time people and places
      Into valleys high and low

Ole war horse
  It is just you and I
    As we ride to an approaching point in time
      Vowing to ride until we die

Not having a destination
  Or one particular place
    Carrying scars in our hearts
      With the almighty wind in our face

I regret I can't make amends
  Dismount and inherit my rightful place
    Climb down from your saddle
      Accepting a woman's warm embrace

She has been left waiting
  In the arms of another man
    Cursing me like the reprobate that I am
      Unable to understand

You can not take a life
  Without giving something in return
    The circle will not be broken
      A lesson I had to learn

I am repaying a debt
  To universal law
    She could only see what was before her
      What was behind she never saw

A glory seeking young rider
  Trained to attack and kill
    Promoted by Uncle Sam
      Who only paid half the bill

A quarter is mine to repay
  Payable only in the passage of hard years
    The other quarter goes to those who care for me
      Payable only in the shedding of bitter tears

For each time I stop to unsaddle midnight
  I look around with caution and care
    Knowing death stalks my back trail
      I can feel his presence there

Hoping one day to catch me off guard
  Where surely I can't win
    Sending my blood back into the earth
      As he does to all mortal men

But for now I am riding tall
  Where fearful men dread
    Sanctioning an all but lost cause
      Here among the walking dead

I have committed a bunch of errors
  But forgiveness will not come to me
    Until I acknowledge every sin I have committed
      Which I know can never be

I was not one of the good
  I was one of the best
    Killing was my special domain
      With a body count high above the rest

Now I ride the earth in somber vigilance
  Searching for an honorable end
    Which seems to be getting more elusive
      It would be easier to grasp a passing wind

Still it doesn't matter if I was wrong
  It doesn't matter if I was right
    With no one beside me I ride the dark horse
    The bronco busting back of midnight

Buck Davis

IF THE TRUTH BE TOLD

THE UNIVERSE IS UNFOLDING
SHIELDED BY YEARLY SEQUENCE
TO IMPART A NATURAL TERRESTRIAL SECRET
YIELDING A GRAIN OF HAPPINESS
FOR EVERY UNSELFISH THOUGHT

FOR ONLY IN THE SELF DELUSIONARY PRACTICES
OF VAIN PURSUITS AND IDOLATRY ARE WE
CONFUSED
AND ONLY WITH THE INTERCESSION OF ABSOLUTE
TRUTHFULNESS
TO OUR SELVES THEN UNTO OTHERS
WILL CALM RETURN YOU TO YOUR SOURCE

UNDERSTANDING IS THE KEY
KNOWLEDGE IS THE DOOR
WISDOM IS THE OBTAINABLE
THROUGH SACRIFICIAL INDULGENCES

AS THE ROOT IS RELATED TO THE TREE
AS SOIL IS RELATED TO THE FARMER
AS WATER IS RELATED TO FISH
YOU ARE RELATED TO ME
ESSENTIAL ... ESSENCE

THAT WHICH WAS BEFORE
ONLY LEFT FRAGMENTS OF WHAT WAS
THAT WHICH IS NOW
IS FREE OF THAT WHICH WILL BE
IF THE BEING IS AUTONOMOUS

GUILT IS BORN OF GRIEF
LOANED BY THE WOES OF SORROW
IN EFFORTS TO REPARATE A DEED
DESTINED TO BE UNDONE

JEALOUSY ENVY AND BIGOTRY
ARE ALL BORN OF FEAR
AFRAID OF THAT WHICH NEVER WAS
AFRAID OF THAT WHICH NEVER WILL BE
UNLESS THE CARRIER GIVES IT AN UNWANTED
BEGINNING

IN THE TRIANGULAR DESIGN OF OUR EXISTENCE
THREE FORCES DOMINANTLY PREVAIL
NEUTRALITY IS THE LEAST OF THE THREE
FOR IT OFFERS NOTHING MUCH
AND ACCEPTS LESS THAN IT OFFERS

THAT IN ITSELF ALLOWS MORE FREEDOM
THAN ANY LEGAL DOCUMENT
HIPPOCRATIC OATH OR SECTARIAN DECREE
SUPPOSEDLY CAST BY SHADOWS CENTURIES OLD
WHY AREN'T THEY FORGOTTEN LIKE THEIR
INVENTORS
BECAUSE USEFUL PURPOSES HAVE NO CLAIM OF ITS
OWN

SO IN RETROSPECT ALL THAT I AM BEGINS WITH
YOU...
AND ENDS IN OBLIVION...

BUCK DAVIS

THE SHADES OF EMENDATION

MY DEAREST IMMANENCY
IN YOUR ABSENCE I SEEK THE ONE I LOVE SO
WITH ENDLESS LIMITATIONS OF SACRED BOUNTIES
I'VE LET MYSELF GO

AWAY FROM THE DELUSIONS OF DESIRING
ANYTHING SAVE YOUR PRECIOUS NAME
AND AWAY FROM THOSE WHO WOULD NOT HONOR
YOU
FOR SURELY THEY CAN NOT BE HELD TO BLAME

INSTEAD OF A REALM OF UTMOST CONTENTMENT
AFFIRMATION OF YOUR THOUGHTS I HAVE READ
AND LIKE A BIRD ALOFT A TREE
BEING SHELTERED AND FED

MY DARLING – MY HEART – MY SELF
I CAN SENSE YOUR MEANINGFUL YEARNING
BUT IT HAS BEEN WILLED YOUR PRESENCE BE
ABSENT
IN THIS SELECT TIME OF MY LEARNING

YOU HAVE ENLIGHTENED MINE INNER EYES
YOU ARE A SOURCE OF WONDERMENT TO MY IDLE
EARS
YOU ARE A FITTING MEDIARY TO SUPPLEMENT
THESE HEART-BREAKING YEARS

YOU ARE MY GIFT FROM OUR FATHER
AND THOU SHALL NOT BE ABUSED
FOR IF I CAN'T MAINTAIN MY SUBSTANTIALNESS
THIS INSTRUCTION I WILL HAVE REFUSED

BUT THINK NOT LESS OF ME
LET YOUR HEART BE AS A FIRE SET ABLAZE
KNOWING THIS IS OUR FATHER'S WILL
TO TEST OUR EPHEMERAL PHASE

MY PEN CAPTURES MANY THINGS THE MIND
STRUGGLES TO COMPREHEND
AND NO MERE WORDS CAN SAY
BUT FOR IT WRITE THE ABSOLUTE TRUTH OF MY
FEELINGS
IT WOULD LEAD YOUR EARS ASTRAY

CAN ANY HUMAN EYES SEE THROUGH STONE
TO THE INNER CORE
CAN ANY HUMAN SPEAK OF SOMETHING
APPRECIATIVELY
THEY HAVE NOT EXPERIENCED BEFORE

FOR IF ONE CAN
I MUST SEEK HIM OUT
AND THROUGH HIS UNIQUE GIFT OF THIS WISDOM
I WILL ASK HIM TO BE MY SCOUT

BUT UNTIL I FIND SUCH A ONE
I WILL ADHERE TO GOD'S UNSEEN EYE
CONTENTMENT REST UPON ME
AS THE HANDS OF TIME RUSHETH ME BY

BUCK DAVIS

REPETITIOUS

FROM THE PRAIRIES OF THE PAST
TO THE DAWN THE FUTURE MADE
WITH LARGE AND SMALL POLITICAL JOKERS
ALL ALONG THE THE MOVING ARCADE

THE SOCIAL MASK ADJUSTED
THE PERSONALITY SNUGLY IN PLACE
THE PERFORMANCE AWAITS US
AS WE INTERACT WITHIN THE HUMAN RACE

BUBBLES OF LESSENING HOPES
TO RISE AND BURST AGAINST THE SKY
LEAVING A SATURINE LEGACY OF HISTORY
THE OMNIBUS AND COMPATIBLE LIE

VARIOUS CONSTRUCTS OF REALITY
SIMILAR GAMES ON STAGE
MULTIPLE MODELS TO EMULATE
WHICH IS FASHIONABLE IN THIS DAY AND AGE

THE SANDS OF TIME
CONTINUE TO DRIFT IN THE CHANGING WIND
CARRYING THE COMEDY AND TRAGEDY
WE ALL ARE PRESENTLY INVOLVED IN

ON BROOMTAIL LUCK AND CHANCE PHENOMENA
WE ARE WHAT WE HAVE BECOME
OUR PAST TIMES OUR FUTURE
EQUALS OUR PRESENT DAILY SUM

DUTY IS THE FIRST INSTRUMENT
IN OUR GOVERNMENT'S MARCH UPON DEATH
FANATICAL LEADERS ENDORSING DISUNION
WITH BOMBS AND BULLETS LEAPING FROM THEIR
BREATH

HONOR IS THE SECOND INSTRUMENT
IN OUR GOVERNMENT'S COHESIVE HOLD
IT WILL BIND ONE TO THE LUDICROUS
MAKING MINDLESS MINIONS MARCH AND PRETEND
TO BE BOLD

NATIONALISM IS THE THIRD AND FINAL INSTRUMENT
IN OUR GOVERNMENT'S DESIRE TO INTERCEDE
SPECIAL INTEREST GROUPS WILL TELL US
WHETHER BUSH PEROT OR CLINTON IS FIT TO LEAD

THE CIRCLE WILL NOT BE BROKEN
THE ROOT IS MUCH TOO DEEP
THE PAST WILL BECOME THE FUTURE
BETWEEN THE ISLES OF SLEEP

BUCK DAVIS

In+fidelis YEARNING

RISING SLOWLY MORNINGS AWAKEN
  SOUND HEART DISPELS HOURLY GLOOM
    PRACTICED ROUTINES HABITUALIZE VOCATION
    MONOTONOUS EMOTIONS LARGELY LOOM

YEAR IN YEAR OUT
  THE HANDS OF TIME TURN
    DAY IN DAY OUT
      UNSPENT PASSIONS BURN

IN THE BEGINNING INNOCENCE REIGNED
  LIFE WAS SWELL
    KNOWLEDGE WAS OBTAINED FROM THE TREE OF
  LIFE
      PLUMMETING FROM LOFTY HEIGHTS LOVE FELL

BETRAYAL RAN RAMPANT
  BUSTED ASPIRATIONS TOOK WINGS AND FLEW
    INDISCRETIONS FLOATED IN MID-SENTENCE
    FROM THE OUTSIDE A COLD WIND BLEW

TO THE PRINCIPLE OF AN OATH
  YOU TOOK A BELEAGUERED STAND
    FOR BETTER OR WORSE
      WITHIN THE REALM OF A GOLD BAND

BITTER IS THE TASTE OF DISAPPOINTMENT
  ACKNOWLEDGING AN UN-REPENTED SIN
    SUPPORTED BY A YOKE AROUND INTENTIONS
    THREATENING TO BRING JEALOUSY IN

CHAINED TO RETREATING MEMORIES
  LINKED WITH EVENTS OF YESTERDAY
    OF YOUTHFUL AND LOVING MOONS ENCIRCLED BY
    SADNESS
      TIME TOOK PAINFULLY AWAY

FLEETING THOUGHTS RACE RAPIDLY
  DURING MOMENTS SPENT UTTERLY ALONE
    IMPRESSIONS COLD AS A DEAD MAN'S BREATH
      CHILLS THE MARROW OF THE BONE

RESIGNED TO LIVE FOR THE LIGHT
  EMANATING FROM BEHIND SPIRITUAL EYES
    IMMUNE TO EXTERNAL DISTRACTIONS
      AND THE DOUR SOUND OF RHYMATIC LIES

  BOTTLED UP INSIDE THE BOUNDARIES OF SANITY
    TIGHT AS A DRUM
      UNRESPONSIVE TO SENSUAL INITIATIVE
        COPULATION MANIFESTED PRONE AND NUMB

COVERED IN THE EVENINGS
  BY THE DARK OF DUST
    THE INNER SOUL ESCAPES CONSCIOUSNESS
      TO HIDE FROM MORTAL LUST

ONLY TO RETURN TO A DAILY PRAYER
  THAT THE FLAME OF HOPE IS NOT TRULY DEAD
    PATIENCE AND PERSEVERANCE WILL BRING LOVE
      ABUNDANTLY TO A LONELY BED

BUCK DAVIS

ALL ROADS LEAD TO FREEDOM

I welcome you children of the night
Gathered here
Your madnesses have descended upon you
In a thousand circles of fear

What lies do you tell yourself
When loneliness visits your cell
To keep you smiling and complacent
In society's deep bottomless hell

You young lions who once stood
With a mighty roar
Now reduced to paupers of infamy
Entertaining thoughts of nevermore

Here in this realm of big dreams
And cramped space
Stands the imprisoned predator
Vanishing without leaving a trace

A scrub that dared to grow
In a meadow green
Dared to question Authority's prerogative
Branded vile gruesome and obscene

Come back little ones
Return I say
To yourselves
The person of yesterday

Wake up – stretch
Rise from the sleeper's bed
Breathe inspirational thoughts
It's time to reclaim the walking dead

All doors lead to freedom
Just be careful where you step
Because if you should fall
It's there you will be kept

Not by a concrete wall
Or a steel bar
You will remain where you fall
Because of who you are

Those of you that are passing through
Look around and remember these armed and childish men
For like them or not
They are letting you pass safely through Satan's den

THE RECKONING OF ALL ETERNITY

DURING THE DECREPIT BILLOWING OF TIME
  MANY GENERATIONS HAS PASSED OVER THE ROCK
   IF THERE IS ANY THAT SPEAKS ITS DIALECT
    MANY ILLUSIVE MYSTERIES IT WOULD HASTEN TO
    UNLOCK

IT IS A PRODUCT OF NATURE
  ONE SELDOM SEES
   SUBLIMED BY GROWTH AND FOLIAGE
    UNTO THE CHOSEN IT PURPOSES IT FREES

ADAM AS ANY MAN TODAY LEFT HIS GARDEN OF
EDEN
  NOT IN HAPPINESS OR DISPLEASURE
   INSTEAD IN TEARFUL MOURN
    FOR HE APPRECIATED AND TASTED NOT OF GOD'S
    TREASURE

HIS MERE ATONEMENT OF CRAVING
  SPOILED HIS PARADISE MUCH TO FAR
   FORGETTING ALL ENTRUSTED UNTO HIM
    HE REACHED INTO EMPTY SPACE TO PLUCK A STAR

ANY MAN THAT LOVETH CREATIONS
  THROUGH HIM GOD HAVE ENDOWED
   SHALL SURELY SMELL OF HIS OWN STENCH
    AND HIS SOUL IS BENEATH THAT WHICH IS
    PLOWED

TO SANCTION THYSELF
  MORE THAN THE ALMIGHTY HAS GIVEN TO THEE
   WILL ALWAYS BE LOST IN HELL'S FIRE
    AND THEIR SINS WILL PAY THE TOLLS OF THE
    BURNING SEA

AND OUR ALMIGHTY FATHER
  WILL CONTINUE TO REIGN THROUGH-OUT ETERNITY
    SO IT HAS BEEN
     SO IT SHALL BE
       BEYOND ANY ILLUSIONS OF HEAVEN OR HELL
        TO THE RECKONING OF ALL ETERNITY

I HAVE COME TO SPEAK OF MY FATHER
  I SEEK REFUGE FROM NO MAN ENTERING THE SEA OF
  FIRE
     LISTENS TO TRANSCENDAL IDLEMENT OF TIME
       WHERE HIS HEART AND SOUL THUS RETIRE

IF A MOUNTAIN ABOVE THE CLOUDS
  WITH A MYRIAD OF HEIGHTNESS
    CRUMBLED PARALLEL THE GROUND
      THEY   WOULD   STILL   MISS   MY   FATHER'S
      BRIGHTNESS

TAKE CALCULATED HEED FROM THIS POINT HERE
  ABOUT LIMITED THOUGHTS OF A REALM BEYOND
    BECAUSE IF THOU IS NOT PERMISSIVE ENOUGH
      YOUR GRIEF SHALL DERIVE FROM THINGS YOU
      HOLD FOND

IN THE FORM OF ACHIEVEMENT OR AUTHORITY
  MAKE THOU FORSAKE ONE DEAR SOUL
    THE WANT OF FORGIVENESS WILL SLASH AT THEE
      AGAIN AND AGAIN UNTOLD

FOR HE THAT HAS THE RIGHT TO MAKE JUDGMENT
  DO SO WITH OUT GOD'S AMAZING GRACE
    THE HEINOUS MARK OF SATAN WILL ILLUMINATE
      THIS MAN'S FACE

HE WHO TAKE AWAY YOUR BIRTH KNOWLEDGE
  AND CONCEAL YOUR GOD GIVEN BIRTHRIGHT
    KNOW HIM WELL IN HIS SHADOWY EXISTENCE
      HE COMES WITH CONFUSION NOT TRUTH IN THE
      LIGHT

HE THAT BUILDS CASTLES
  FROM ANOTHER MAN'S SWEAT
    SHALL DIE THIRSTING
      IN DEATH HE CAN'T QUENCH OR FORGET

HE THAT CURSES YOU
  AND DENIES THAT YOU ARE HIS BROTHER
    WILL NOT BE ABLE TO LOVE HIMSELF
      NOR ANY OTHER

HE OR SHE THAT PUT ASIDE THEIR MOTHER AND
FATHER
  AT AN OLD AND GRACEFUL AGE
    WILL NOT BE FOUND IN THE BOOK OF LIFE
      NO NOT ON ANY PAGE

NO MAN CAN SERVE TWO MASTERS
  NOT WHEN OUR FATHER IS THE HOST
    YOU WILL LOVE ONE AND HATE THE OTHER
      DEPENDING ON WHICH ONE PAYS THE MOST

SO ON THIS THANKSGIVING DAY
  LET US GIVE CREDIT WHERE CREDIT IS DUE
    OUR FATHER WILL NOT OVERBURDEN US
      HE CARRIES THEM WHEN WE ARE NOT ABLE TO

SO BE THANKFUL HE WILL NEVER LEAVE US
  TO THE INHUMAN TREATMENT OF PHARAOH'S KIND
    WHO ALSO PRAY TO HIM IN DARKNESS
      LIKE HIS EYES ARE BLIND

I KNOW THERE IS SOME PRESENT
  WHO WILL DISPUTE THE THINGS I HAVE SAID
    BUT OUR HEAVENLY FATHER DOESN'T CHARGE FOR
    LAND OR BLESSINGS
      OTHERWISE WE ALL WOULD BE IN THE SEA OR
      DEAD

BUT FOR LIVING
  AND BEING SPIRITUALLY FREE
    YOU CAN GIVE THANKS NOW
      OR FACE JUDGMENT AT THE RECKONING OF ALL
      ETERNITY

                              BUCK DAVIS

ONCE UPON A TIME IN THE LAND OF NOD

Unto an unGodly time
  Unto a land that never should have been
    Paid for with the innocent blood
      Of the Great grandchildren of the first freed men

The Keys of the kingdom
  Were finally handed down
    To the lowest of the earth
      Comes the inheritance of the Lord's Crown

Ris-ing from the Earth
  To initially touch the skies
    Spirits journeying home
      To a Love that never dies

Two men in one soul
  Battles to be one
    The first seeks wisdom
      The second lust for more fun

The first knows where he is going
  Wisdom directs his every step
    He doesn't have all the keys
      So he goes continually where the Keys are kept

The second wants pleasure
  Whether it comes from money, women, men or cars
    He has sold his birthrights
      For a dream on unreachable stars

That corner of his mind
  Where only the foolish would dread
    He joins with other corruptibles
      Communing with the living dead

We are the Great grandchildren
  Of the first freed men
    The first experiments of cloning
      No race will accept us in

Our uniqueness is vividly discernable
  Every door before Us will not yield
    We must bring the past to the present
      For this purpose Christ is Our best shield

Who knows which house Christ built
  When they all are standing tall
    Which one houses the Good Shepard
      How many will know Him or will answer His call

The roof is leaking
  Raindrops splatter on the floor
    It moves from corner to corner
      No place is dry anymore

The roof being the plains of illusion
  Where brothers indulge themselves into unsterile things
    The floor is our heritage foundations
      Wet with the cruelty disbelief brings

The walls have boards missing
  Anyone can look straight in
    Suspicion rides upon everyone
      Especially your best friend

Your enemies can't harm you
  They are from without
    It is your friend whom you trust
      Who will signal your fall with a traitorous shout

The walls being strengths
  Real numbers in life's game
    Be careful to him who stands beside you
     Who else can tell from where you came

The benches are hard
  Its an uncomfortable way to sit
    Dressed in the best disguise
     Scoring another hit

The benches are stubbornness
  To go your own way
    The clothes is pride
    It an uneventful day

The house need repairs
  But first let Us Clean it up inside
    Truth will wash fallacies away
     Leaving no crevice for dirt to hide

Love will cover the leaky roof
  Brotherhood will make the floor dry
    Who can cross over Heaven's Gate
     Without first stooping to meet the Most High

Our time has come
  For the Bilalians to be great
    Only We can stop the inevitable
    By predestination its Our fate

WE are our worst enemy
  In the person of I
    Leave it and come up to the mountain
    It is time your soul was taught to fly

Over needs
  Over joys
    Over pleasures
      Over toys

Over desires
  Over lust
    Over charities
      Over Trust

The sleepers are sleeping
  Let them lay
    Ignorance may be blissful
      It is nothing but a stumbling block thrown in the way

The enemy is entrenched around the throne
  To sever the seed's core
    To erase the knowledge of our enslavement
      To pretend like it doesn't exist any more

It doesn't matter what method is used
  Whether it's drugs, uniforms or sports it's still the same
    We know who is really who
      When it's time to kneel and call His name

                    Buck Davis

EXILED

UNREHEARSED INTERACTIONS
REACTS TO ETERNAL SOUND
IN SLEEP BEYOND SOCIETAL CONTROLS
TO A SECTOR RESERVED AS COMMON GROUND

THIS MYSTERIOUS ANTIDOTE
BEGAN IN THE LAND OF NOD
A CLEAR DISPENSATION OF GUILT
ADMINISTERED BY AN ANGRY GOD

NEVER AGAIN TO BE SUMMONED
THE ASSOCIATION BEING RENT
LEFT TO EVOLVE INTO GENERATIONS OF
SLEEPWALKERS
BECOMING THE NIGHTMARES BEING SPENT

INTEREST COMPOUNDS EQUITY
TIME IS MODIFIED BY LAWFUL LORE
THE MARKET-PLACE IS STILL HELD CAPTIVE
BY THE DESCENDANTS OF THOSE WHO HELD IT
BEFORE

AGGREGATE DEMANDS ON MONOGRAMMED TIDINGS
ILLUMINE THE THE NEON WAY
TO A PATH WITHIN A PASSING MOMENT
STOLEN FROM ACCOMPLISHMENTS OF YESTERDAY

DEEP IS THE DEPTHS OF THE OBSCURE
BETWEEN THE PAGES OF HISTORY
WHEN SLEEP IS THE GUARDIAN OF THE DOOR
TO AN UNHOLY MYSTERY

BUCK DAVIS

FRIEND OR FOE

With all the humility
  Shown to a guest in your beloved home
    With temperance extending beyond these boundaries
      To the habitual haunts you roam

With the hatred and anger
  A known killer must possess
    The courage of a lion and cunning of a feline
      Your enemies must test

Hold in one hand your goodness
  Hold in the other your faults
    Give freely from your good hand
      In your bad hand the giving halts

A friend of my friend
  Is a friend of mine
    A friend of my enemy
      No greater foe I can hope to find

In the ordering of men
  Opposites will certainly repel
    To the peace of heaven's norm
      Or the furies offered from hell

To be a collector of honey
  You must frequent with the bees
    To run with a pack of dogs
      You must expect to gather their fleas

The true worth of a man
  Is not measured in his size
    It is in his strict attention to personal management
      Dependent upon how much acreage his mouth buys

A word given and kept
 Is not a piece of cake
  It entails burdens and responsibilities
   Only a friend is willing to make

In our collective community
 There are millions of men
  With only a solitary few
   Worthy of being called a friend

For every man is my natural enemy
 Until I can see his hand
  A well earned truth
   Spoken in every land

To show little faith
 To the reasoning of your instinctive mind
  Leads to eventual ruin
   Associating obviously with the wrong kind

Many men has fallen
 Trusting not of themselves but the unknown
  Like the leaves that fell last autumn
   They are forgotten and gone

The parable here is two fold
 The blind can not see and needs help
  So he carries the lame and uses his eyes
   To direct his every step

To help or befriend an enemy
 Is an error only a food would make
  For he will bite the hand that fed him
   As surely as a snake

Buck Davis

THE STALKER

I HAVE BEEN TOUCHED
BY NONE OTHER THAN DEATH
AS HE BREATHED ON MY FRIEND
WALKING ON MY LEFT

HIS STEALTH UPON A CHOSE ONE
IS BETTER THAN I HAVE EVER SEEN
HIS MOVEMENTS SO PRECISE
HIS BLOWS SO MEAN

THERE IS NO RETURN
FROM THE TRIP HE BRING
YOU NEVER SEE THE SHINY NEW HEARSE
OR HEAR THE CHOIR SING

YOU NEVER SEE YOUR REMAINS
LAID TO FINALLY REST
YOU DON'T FEEL THE COSMETIC THREAD IN YOUR
FACE
OR YOUR HANDS FOLDED ACROSS YOUR CHEST

WHEN DEATH STEPS TO A PERSON
HE IS GOD-AWFUL QUICK
THERE IS NO TIME FOR A DECISION
NO TIME TO CHOOSE OR PICK

LIFE IS FINISHED
WHEN HIS WORK IS DONE
ON TO ANOTHER CHOSEN PERSON
WHO CAN'T HIDE OR RUN

ONCE DEATH HAS TOUCHED A SOUL
HE NEVER GOES AWAY
LURKING AROUND THE CORNER OF MIDNIGHT
TO STEAL LIFE FROM ANOTHER DAY

HE WALKS WITH ME
AS WE WALK IN STEP
HE TALKS WITH ME
ABOUT APPOINTMENTS HE ALREADY KEPT

THE REASON HE ACCEPTS MY FRIENDSHIP IS
I SHOW HIM NO FEAR
EVERY CONSCIOUS MOMENT IS MINE
UNTIL HE TAKES ME AWAY FROM HERE

HIS DISGUISE DOES NOT MATTER
OR WHO EVER HE CARES TO SEND
HE KNOWS WHILE I WALK THIS EARTH
I WALK WITH HIM AS MY FRIEND

AFTER BEING TOUCHED
YOU ARE NEVER THE SAME
YOU HAVE NO TIME FOR THE MEDIOCRITIES OF
TYRANTS
OR ANY OTHER SILLY ASSED GAME

FROM THE MOMENT OF BIRTH
DEATH STALKS OUR TRAIL
THE BEST STALKER IN CREATION
IT IS IMPOSSIBLE FOR HIM TO FAIL

BUCK DAVIS

THE LIE

Spewed from frothing lips
Moving on thin air
The lie hungereth to be borne
Honesty beware

The specific evil
Only mankind can invent
For mischief or deception
To undo the truth of an event

Like little babies
Into the world they arrive
Growing bigger and bigger
Eating truths to survive

Begun around a morsel of truth
To enhance belief
Empty as an open grave
Bringing death not relief

Tittle tattle tale
Joking playing white lie
Traps to ensnare the gullible
With the bonus of not having to ask why

In a lie
The spirit begins to kill itself
Eating at all the truths
With lies to restock the mental shelf

To be used habitually
Like a loaded gun
The real last fast draw
Capable of killing anyone

The spirit can not live
In the body of a liar
It would be easier to believe an elephant
Can be taught to walk a high wire

A lie is the beginning
An instrument to set the pace
A method to open other doors
Behind a smiling face

A ruse to gather trusting souls
With a gesture of innocent pleas
To slowly wither their resistance
Down around their bended knees

BUCK DAVIS

LIFE'S CYCLE

WHO KNOWS WHAT TIME
WHETHER DAY OR NIGHT
WE WILL LEAVE THIS WORLD
SUMMONED BY A FLASH OF LIGHT

WHO KNOWS WHO WILL BE FIRST
OR WHO WILL BE LAST
WHETHER THE PASSING WILL BE SLOW
OR MUCH TOO FAST

WILL IT BE AN OLD ONE
WHO HAVE LIVED TO SEE THOSE GOLDEN YEARS
ONE READY TO ACCEPT THE ETERNAL REST
AND JOURNEY BEYOND THEIR FEARS

WILL IT BE ONE SO TENDERLY YOUNG
ONE WHO BARELY LIVED AT ALL
SEEMS LIKE YESTERDAY LEAVING THEIR MOTHER'S
BREAST
NEVER AGAIN TO HEAR NATURE'S CALL

THE GRIM REAPER PASSES AMONGST US
WITH HIS SCYTHE CLUTCHED IN HIS FIST
SEARCHING FOR HIS SCHEDULED PATRONS
ON HIS TIME-APPOINTED LIST

EVENTUALLY WE ALL WILL GO
ON THIS PASSING TIDE
TO GLORIFY OUR BEING
DEATH WILL ABIDE

NOT WITH SHALLOW TEARS
OR MISSPENT GRIEF
BUT WITH EARTHLY FRAGRANCES
SALUTING OUR MORTAL RELIEF

FRIENDS AND LOVED ONES
MUST CONTINUE TO LIVE ON
CLINGING TO THE LIVING
THE DEAD BECOME SHORT SHADOWS AFTER THEY
ARE GONE

LOVE EMBRACES LIFE
SORROW CLUTCHES FOR THE DEAD
LOVE IS LETTING GO
SORROW IS MISERY BEING SELFISHLY FED

SO WHO TRULY KNOWS
THE ANSWER TO WHY
NOT ONE BUT...
WE WERE ALL BORN TO DIE

MOTHER FATHER SON DAUGHTER
ONLY CHILD
HERE TODAY GONE TOMORROW
WE HELD THEM FOR A SHORT WHILE...

BUCK DAVIS

ROAD SIGNS

Into our lives people come
Some stay some go
The ones that stay are for real
The others are only show

We are drawn to each other
Beyond societal notions of peers
For reasons of love and trust
For reasons of doubt and fears

For the reasons of love
It is to give without expectation of return
It is the ability to teach love
While maintaining the eagerness to learn

For the reason of trust
It is to gain a newfound friend
To share an abundance of experiences
Or tales spun upon the wind

For the reason of doubt
It is a need to belong
A wish to be special in someone's eyes
A melody in someone's song

For the reason of fear
Doesn't mean we are not strong
Kindness is often mistaken for weakness
And what starts out good sometimes becomes wrong

Traveling down life's highway
We see the good and the bad
Relationships we currently have
Relationships we could have had

We learn to take each mistake
And use it as a tool
Our mistakes are our textbooks
Understanding the gist of our school

With love trust doubt and fear
I have come to you
My heart and conscious is clear
In expectation of something new

My ears are listening
My eyes are opened wide
To climb mountains of passions
To envision the other side

I hope you fully understand
What these few lines meant
Understand them you understand me
Totally one hundred per cent

Buck Davis

CONCLUSION

I would like to thank you for your time and energy spent trying to understand all I have written. I know it wasn't easy. If you have gained anything at all, then it is a blessing upon my head. If ever there was a prodigal son, then I am he.

Also I would like to say that nothing is immediate. Not your birth, nor your death, and everything in between is a journey through different realities. The good realities aren't truly good because they are nearly always replaced by not so good ones. The bad realities aren't truly bad because they are nearly always replaced by not so bad ones. It is our view upon these realities and how we react upon them that is of consequence.

I now leave you in a better state than I found you, hopefully. If you learned nothing else, You have learned that the highway of life is full of fools. Some just foolish and some with extremely good talents going to waste. And I, am chief among them...

The author was born on May 7, 1949. He was a high school dropout who entered the U.S. Military at age seventeen and fought in Viet Nam with the 101st Airborne Infantry Division. After seven years in the Military, the author refused to return to Viet Nam, went A.W.O.L., and was discharged from the Military. Broken in heart and spirit, he turned to drugs and eventually crime. The author has spent over twenty years in prisons and has used this time to write and reflect upon how he may now serve society. He is currently serving time at The Federal Correctional Institution at Allenwood and expects to be released soon. This book is a demonstration of using this time constructively for his and society's benefit.